Travelling SOLO to France

France

Written and illustrated
by Bettina Guthridge

SOLOS

Southwood Books Limited
3-5 Islington High St
London N1 9LQ

First published in Australia by Omnibus Books 2001
This edition published in the UK under licence from
Omnibus Books by
Southwood Books Limited 2002

Cover design by Lyn Mitchell
Typeset by Clinton Ellicott, Adelaide
Printed in Singapore

1 903 207 58 4

A CIP catalogue record for this book is available from
the British Library.

FRANCE

The capital
is Paris.

The money is
the euro.

60 million people
live in France.

The language
is French.

The French flag.

MAP OF FRANCE

ENGLAND

ENGLISH

Mont St Michel

BRITTANY

ATLANTIC OCEAN

Carnac

Loire Ri

River Giron

Lascaux

Pyrénées

SPAIN

ANDORRA

N
W E
S

2

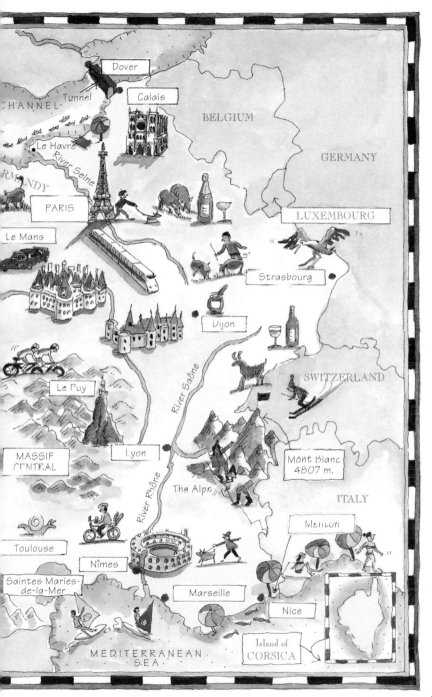

3

France is a large country in Europe.
It has six sides like a hexagon.

It shares its borders with six countries, from Belgium in the north to Spain in the south.

4

The island of Corsica is part of France.

Tourists come here for holidays.

Some towns on the coast can be reached only by boat.

France has snow-capped
mountains, forests,
sandy beaches and
rolling plains.

Loire River

Bay of Biscay

Mont Blanc is the highest
mountain.

The longest river is
the Loire.

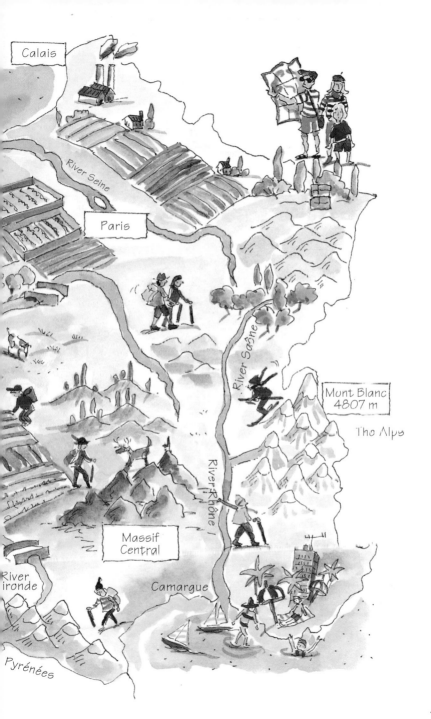

Calais

River Seine

Paris

Mont Blanc
4807 m

The Alps

River Saône

River Rhône

Massif
Central

River
Gironde

Camargue

Pyrénées

7

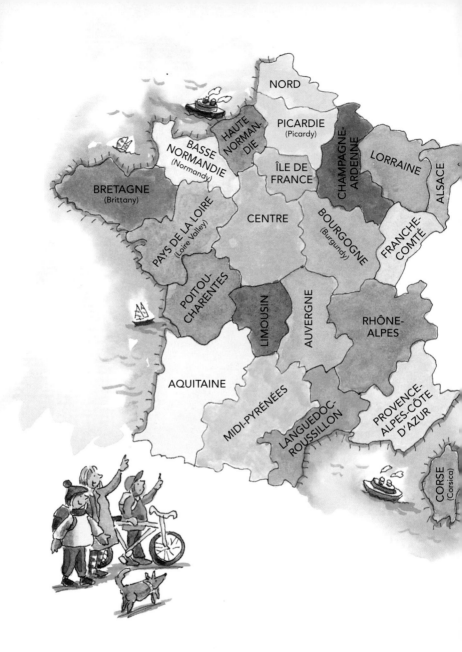

France is divided into many regions.

BRITTANY

PROVENCE

BURGUNDY

PYRÉNÉES

ALSACE

SAVOY ALPS

MASSIF CENTRAL

People from each region still have their own customs, languages and dress.

Chenonceaux is built across a river.

Langeais has terrible dungèons.

Azay-le-Rideau was used as a hunting lodge.

Chambord has
365 chimneys,
440 rooms and
65 staircases.

France is a very modern country, but it
has a long history. Along the Loire
River are many beautiful castles. Kings
and queens from long ago lived here.

Many castles have
beautiful gardens laid out
in patterns. Villandry has
the most famous garden.

In the Loire Valley there are also houses built in soft limestone caves. These caves are cut into the side of a hill or dug underground.

Some people still live in them. These houses are warm in winter and cool in summer.

The caves are a good place to grow
mushrooms and to store wine.

There are ancient monuments in France. At Carnac in Brittany there are lines and circles of stones built many hundreds of years ago. Some of these stones stood up to 4 metres high.

Some stones stand alone.

These stones marked a burial chamber.

Stones were stood up to form a corridor.

A burial mound was formed from stones and soil.

Why the stones were placed in this way is still a mystery.

Pirates used to sail the rocky coast of Brittany. Bad weather caused many shipwrecks. The Bretons (the people of Brittany) collected pirate treasure as it floated in on the tide.

The church

Towers and high walls protected the island from attack.

Mont St Michel is a tiny island off the coast of Normandy. It was built long ago as an abbey. It was used later as a prison and a fortress.

The island was formed like this.

Long ago there was a hill with a forest.

Sea water swept the trees away.

The hill became an island.

Strong tides move at the speed of a gulloping horse.

Some prisoners jumped to their death from this terrace.

Strong tides and dangerous quicksand stopped prisoners escaping. Today a road joins the island to the mainland. Many tourists come to see it.

In French cities many people live in small apartments. Some have balconies. These buildings often have a courtyard in the middle.

Many apartment buildings have a caretaker.

French people buy their bread fresh every day.

They also like to shop in the many open-air food markets.

Most cities have parks where children can play and relax.

In the country there are
many old towns and villages.
Many have a town or
village square.

People meet
in the square
to chat, to do
their shopping
or to play a
game of *boules*.

The player who
can roll the
boule closest
to the small
wooden ball is
the winner.

The shops close at lunch time. Many people go home to have lunch. For French people, lunch has long been the most important meal of the day.

There are many small farms in France.

French farms produce many different foods.

Wines and cheeses from France are sold all over the world.

Asparagus   Garlic   Plums

Tobacco   Apples   Olives

This is how wine is made.

1. Grapes are picked. Green grapes make white wine. Black grapes make red or white wine.

2. Grape juice is processed and stored in barrels to ferment into wine.

3. Wine is bottled, or stored longer in a cool, dark cellar to develop its flavour.

This is how cheese is made.

1. Rennet and sour milk are added to milk to "separate" it.

2. The liquid (the whey) is drained from the solids (the curds).

3. The curds are shaped in a mould and left to dry and mature.

Over 400 kinds of cheese are made in France.

There are many ways to travel around France.

The first hot air balloon was invented in 1783 by the Montgolfier brothers.

The quickest way around Paris is the underground train called the Métro.

Some entrances to Métro stations are very beautiful.

The *TGV*, a very fast train, travels at speeds of up to 300 kilometres an hour.

The bicycle is still popular in the country.

The Concorde is the world's fastest passenger plane. It cruises at over 2000 kilometres per hour.

The famous Citroen 2CV is called the *deux chevaux* (two horses). It has a two-horsepower engine.

The Channel tunnel carries passengers, cars and goods under the sea between England and France.

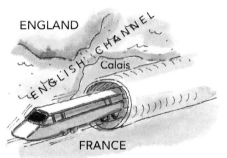

ENGLAND

ENGLISH CHANNEL

Calais

FRANCE

Barges on canals move goods to the port of Le Havre.

Paris is the capital of France. Paris is a beautiful city with many museums, churches, monuments and street cafés.

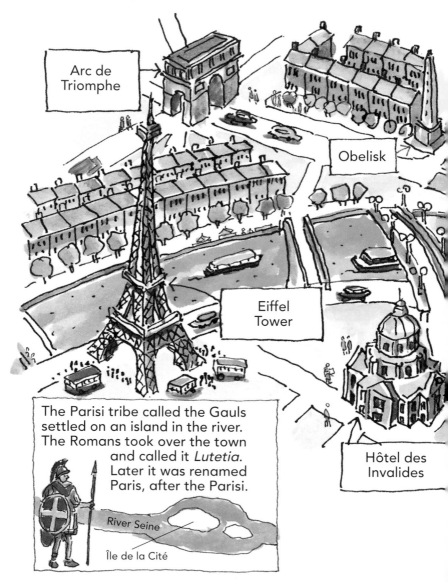

Arc de Triomphe

Obelisk

Eiffel Tower

Hôtel des Invalides

The Parisi tribe called the Gauls settled on an island in the river. The Romans took over the town and called it *Lutetia*. Later it was renamed Paris, after the Parisi.

River Seine

Île de la Cité

The first city was built on an island in the River Seine.

Opera House

Pompidou Centre

Louvre Museum

...ots of ...idges

River Seine

Notre Dame is on an island (Île de la Cité)

Paris is famous for its art and culture. Many artists have lived and worked in Paris.

Claude Monet   Edgar Degas   Raoul Dufy

Today many art works from long ago can be seen at the Louvre Museum.

Many tourists from all over the world come to Paris to see the Louvre. It is the biggest art gallery in the world.

One of the famous paintings in the Louvre is the *Mona Lisa* by Leonardo da Vinci.

Mona Lisa

The Eiffel Tower in Paris was once the tallest building in the world. It was built over 100 years ago.

Gustave Eiffel designed the tower. Another famous design is the structure for the Statue of Liberty in New York.

A French tailor once jumped off the tower using his cape for wings. He was killed.

Now it is visited by many tourists. Some people travel to the top of the tower in a lift. Others climb the stairs.

Level three is 276 metres high and can hold 800 people at a time.

The tower
- is made from 7000 tonnes of iron
- has 2.5 million rivets
- expands in hot weather and contracts in cold weather
- needs 40 tonnes of paint every four years.

Restaurant

Level two is 115 metres high.

Museum

Post office

Level one is 57 metres high.

Outdoor cafés are
an important part
of French life.

People visit cafés to eat, drink, talk to
their friends or just watch the world
go by.

French people love good food. French restaurants and the French style of cooking are world famous.

In the countryside, local foods can be famous too. People travel far to taste special dishes like snails, pigs' trotters and wild game.

At home, food is an important part of family life.

Meals are served with wine and fresh bread.

Different breads have different names.

One type of bread is called a *baguette*.

For the French, breakfast is a simple meal of bread, butter and jam.

There might also be coffee with milk or hot chocolate.

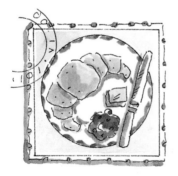

Pastries called *croissants* are often served with coffee for breakfast.

Some children like to dip bread into hot chocolate.

Different regions of France have their own special dishes.

Quiche from
Lorraine

A salad with
olives from
Provence

Beef stew with
wine from
Burgundy

Mussels from
Brittany

Pancakes from
Brittany

Pâté from
Alsace

Black truffles are fungi
that grow underground.
Trained pigs sniff
them out.

Children drink a little
wine with their meals
on special occasions.

In France, children go to school at 8.30 in the morning and finish at 4 o'clock in the afternoon. There are classes on Saturday mornings, but Wednesday afternoon is usually free.

French children work hard at school.

Most children wear jeans and sneakers to school rather than a uniform. They either have lunch at school or go home to eat.

French children play many sports including football, volleyball and basketball.

In winter skiing and skating are also popular.

The French love sport. Many big sporting events are held in France.

Le Mans car race

Monte Carlo rally

The *Tour de France* is a bicycle race across France. It is very hard.

Soccer is very popular in France, but there are many other sports.

Tennis   Soccer   Skiing

Horse-riding   Sailing   Bullfights

Many different people have ruled France.

A long time ago the Romans came to France. They built great bridges, temples and roads. Today some of these buildings can be seen in French towns and cities.

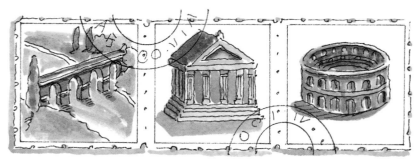

This is an aqueduct. It carried water.

A temple is where people prayed.

Men and animals fought each other in this arena.

Great obelisks were brought from Egypt.

Romans saw plays in outdoor arenas.

Pictures of great battles were carved on arches.

Joan of Arc was a brave young girl
who led an army against the English.
She won an important battle.

Later her enemies handed her over to
the English.

Clovis the
First

Charlemagne

Henry the
Second

France was once ruled by kings.

King Louis the Fourteenth built the
royal palace of Versailles. This was a
huge palace with beautiful fountains
and gardens.

Henry the
Fourth

Louis the
Fourteenth

Louis the
Sixteenth

Louis called himself the Sun King. He
thought he was like the sun that lit
up France.

At the time of Louis the Sixteenth,
many people in France were poor and
hungry. They rose up against the king.

The people took over the Bastille Prison.

This time was called the French Revolution. The king and other rich people had their heads cut off on the guillotine.

Today this column stands where the Bastille Prison used to be. Bastille Day is a holiday in France.

Napoleon Bonaparte was a great soldier. He became a hero of the French people.

Napoleon led his army into war and won great battles. He made himself the emperor of France.

Napoleon's tomb is inside this building in Paris. It is called the Hôtel des Invalides.

People from many different countries live in France now. There are many different religions.

Many Jewish people live in central Paris.

Muslims worship at a mosque.

There are Muslims and Jewish people as well as people who follow other Christian faiths.

Today most French people are Catholics.

French churches and cathedrals are very beautiful buildings.

Gargoyles

"Rose" window
of stained glass

Notre Dame in Paris is a very famous
building. The spire can be seen from a
long way away. There is a famous bell
in the tower.

Stone animals
called gargoyles
kept away evil
spirits.

Stained glass
windows show
stories from
the Bible.

There are
carved figures
on columns and
doorways.

WOLF

HERON

BEAR

WILD BOAR

HARE

Many animals in France are in danger of becoming extinct. This is because much land has been cleared for farming. Today there are reserves to protect wildlife.

Cowboys called *gardiens* look after the horses that graze here.

PIG

FLAMINGO

WILD CAT

FOX

MOLE · STORK · WEASEL · CHAMOIS · HOOPOE · SQUIRREL · BADGER · EAGLE · POLE CAT

The Camargue is a huge marsh land in southern France. Flocks of birds visit these lands. There are pink flamingoes.

Many people come to France to see
fashion created by famous designers.
France is famous for perfumes and
other luxury goods.

Chanel   Dior   Cartier

Extracts from flowers are used in making perfume. In the south of France, fields of lavender and other flowers are grown to make flower oils.

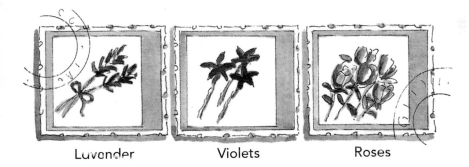

Lavender   Violets   Roses

A perfume may contain as many as 300 different oils. Perfume was first used hundreds of years ago to cover up the smell of leather in gloves.

Henri Matisse

Jean-Jacques
Rousseau

René Descartes

Many important ideas about the way
we live today came from France.

Jean-Jacques Rousseau, Victor Hugo,
and Simone de Beauvoir were famous
writers. René Descartes changed the
history of science. Henri Matisse
changed modern art.

Victor Hugo

Simone de
Beauvoir

General Charles
de Gaulle

General Charles de Gaulle helped
make France a strong country.

Pierre and Marie Curie discovered radium, which is used in X-rays.

The Lumière brothers invented a machine for showing films.

Louis Braille was blind. He invented a way for blind people to read.

France has many festivals.

Bastille Day celebrates the storming of the Bastille during the French Revolution.

At the gypsy festival at Saintes-Maries-de-la-Mer a statue of Saint Sarah is carried into the sea.

Bullfights are held in the old arena.

There are many wine festivals.

At Menton huge sculptures of fruit are made to celebrate the harvest. This model of the Taj Mahal is made of lemons and oranges.

People dress in bright costumes and papier mâché masks at the carnival in Nice.

Children wear special costumes for the *Cornouailles* festival.

Music concerts are held in churches in autumn.

King Louis the Sixteenth and his wife Marie Antoinette had their heads cut off on the guillotine. The man who lowered the blade wore a mask.

Under Paris are tunnels called catacombs. When the Paris cemeteries were full, bones and skulls were stored here.

30,000 tonnes of snails are eaten every year in France.

Hundreds of years ago, a disease called the Black Death killed thousands of people in France. Doctors wore masks and robes to protect them from the disease.

58

Know?

Sewer Tours

Visitors can take a tour through the sewers beneath the city of Paris.

Tintin and *Asterix* are favourite characters from French comics.

TinTin

French people love their dogs. They often take them to restaurants.

Montmartre is the artists' quarter of Paris. Famous artists used to work there.

In Paris in June there is a special waiters' race.

GLOSSARY

abbey ★ building for a group of monks or nuns.

ancient Romans ★ people who lived in Rome over 2000 years ago.

apartment ★ flat or unit.

aqueduct ★ bridge that carried water.

arena ★ place where games were held.

boules ★ game played outside with heavy wood or metal balls.

canal ★ water way dug to carry people and goods between two places.

extinct ★ died out.

festival ★ a time to celebrate and have fun.

French Revolution ★ time in history when the people took power to rule the country away from the king.

gardiens ★ the French name for cowboys in the south of France.

gargoyles ★ ugly human or animal creatures carved from stone used as gutters on very old buildings.

hexagon ★ a shape with six sides.

market ★ place for buying and selling goods.

obelisk ★ four-sided stone monument.

opera ★ play where the words are sung.

palace ★ home for a king or queen.

papier mâché ★ hard material like cardboard made from paper and glue and dried.

quicksand ★ loose wet sand that sucks in anything falling into it.

republic ★ country ruled by the people, not by a king or queen.

Taj Mahal ★ famous building in India.

INDEX